IMAGES
of England

BOWDON AND
DUNHAM MASSEY

Viscount Groby and Lady Jane Grey, the children of the Earl and Countess of Stamford, at Dunham Massey Hall in 1906.

IMAGES
of England

BOWDON AND
DUNHAM MASSEY

Compiled by
Bowdon History Society

TEMPUS

First published 1999, reprinted 2001
Copyright © Bowdon History Society, 1999

Tempus Publishing Limited
The Mill, Brimscombe Port,
Stroud, Gloucestershire, GL5 2QG

ISBN 0 7524 1528 X

Typesetting and origination by
Tempus Publishing Limited
Printed in Great Britain by
Midway Clark Printing, Wiltshire

Bibliography

Bamford, Frank. (1991) *Mansions and Men of Dunham Massey*.

Bayliss, Donald. (ed.) *Altrincham: A History*. Willow Publishing.

Bowdon History Society. *Bowdon Sheaf*.

Chartres, John. (1991) *The Training of World War Two Secret Agents in Cheshire*.

Cox, M. (1995) *William Wood of Bowdon: Champion of 'Climbing Boys'*.
Transactions, Lancashire and Cheshire Antiquarian Society, Vol. 91.

Cox, M., Kemp, P., Trenbath, R. (1994) *Bowdon Hall and its People*.

Figueiredo, P. de C.,Treuherz, R. (eds.) (1988) *Cheshire Country Houses*. Phillimore.

Ingham, Alfred. (1899) *Altrincham and Bowdon*. Second edition.

Kemp, Peter. (1985) *Higher Downs, Altrincham: A Short History*.

Kendrick, Myra. (1996) *Schools in Victorian Bowdon*.

Littler, Joyce. (1993) *The Protectors of Dunham Massey*. Joyce Littler Publications.

The National Trust. (1981) *Dunham Massey*.

The National Trust. (1990) *An Illustrated Souvenir: Dunham Massey, Cheshire*.

Ormerod, George. (1882) *The History of the County Palatine and City of Chester*.
Second edition, revised by T. Helsby.

Sylvester, D., Nulty, G. (eds.) (1958, revised in 1966) *The Historic Atlas of Cheshire*.
Cheshire Community Council.

Trenbath, R. (1984) *The Rebuilding of Bowdon Parish Church*.

Contents

The Polygon shops, Bowdon, en fête to welcome the return of the Stamfords. The shops in the background include a grocer, chemist, fruiterer, confectioner, bootmaker, photographer and post office. (Photograph by Estelle, c. 1906.)

Acknowledgements

This book was compiled by Douglas Rendell, Ronald Trenbath and Chris Hill with the assistance of Marjorie Cox and Valerie Trenbath. The following members of Bowdon History Society also contributed to the publication: Edwin Chalmers, Beryl Chartres , Myra Kendrick, Charles Metcalfe, Susan Sanderson.

Acknowledgement must also be made to Canon Maurice Ridgway, former vicar of Bowdon and founder member of Bowdon History Society, for help and encouragement in the early stages of the project, and also to the late Professor Barker and the late Henry Ward whose initial work must be recorded.

The authors gratefully acknowledge permission to reproduce illustrations and material from the following: Mr T. Bailey, Mrs R. Blakeney-Flyn, Mr and Mrs Chester, Mr E. Clark, Mr T. Clarke, Denton Local History Society, The Documentary Photograph Archive, Hale Civic Society, Mr A. Hewitt, Mrs H. Heyworth, HM Stationery Office, Mr R. Hughes, Mrs M. King, Mr B. Knowles, Manchester City Council, Mrs J. Monkhouse, The National Trust, Royal Northern College of Music, Sale Local Studies, Mr G. Sheppard, Mr N. Spilsbury.

Bowdon History Society also wishes to acknowledge the assistance afforded by local residents who donated photographs or gave permission for their houses to be photographed.

Introduction

Bowdon and Dunham Massey are situated in North Cheshire on either side of the main road between Chester and Manchester. They can be found to the south of the Mersey Valley, which divides the historic County Palatine of Chester from Lancashire. In AD 1000 the two districts formed a manorial estate which developed during the eighteenth century through salt working, advances in agriculture, forestry and improved transport.

In the early Victorian era the building of a railway helped to link the area with the developing industrial belt of South Lancashire, derisively named 'Cottonopolis'. This led to the creation of a unique suburban community for industrialists, or 'Cottontots', where they could escape from the squalor which they had created, live in elegant refinement and entertain their taste for cultural activities. The deer park and estate at neighbouring Dunham Massey provided a venue for healthy exercise.

The economic depression that followed the First World War led to a decline in Bowdon's living standards, with consequent urban decay which lasted for forty years, until the revitalisation of the North West as a centre of technology and the reoccupation of Bowdon by technocrats in the late twentieth century.

Some of Bowdon's early Victorian residents were pioneering photographers who recorded buildings which have since disappeared or been altered beyond recognition. In previous centuries, local landowners commissioned paintings showing early features in graphic detail. In this book the Bowdon History Society, which was founded in 1979, aims to illustrate life in the area during the various stages of development over 1,000 years, using material obtained from research with selected pictures.

The deer park at Dunham Massey is of Saxon origin. Although there have been others in the area, the park is the only one to survive for the whole millennium. The herd, which consists exclusively of fallow deer, was originally kept for hunting. At one time Dunham Massey had the second largest herd in the country after the royal deer at Windsor.

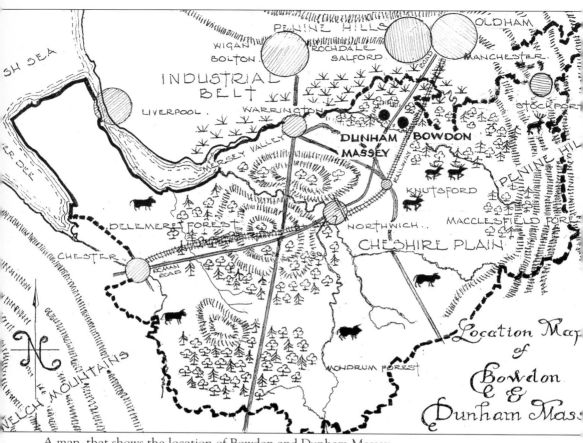

A map that shows the location of Bowdon and Dunham Massey.

One
The de Masseys

In AD 1000 Bowdon, or Bogedone as it was then named, and the adjoining village of Dunham were two, small, isolated settlements on high ground in the north of the Roman province that later became Cheshire. The hill was surrounded by the impenetrable marshland of the River Mersey Valley to the north and the River Bollin Valley to the south. These separated it from the dense oak forests of the Cheshire plain and the scattered settlements of people from mixed ethnic, but primarily Celtic stock, to the south.

Most of the land in the district, including much of that in adjoining Bochelau (Bucklow), was held by Alweard, a Saxon lord. Alweard also owned a herd of deer, which are still a feature of Dunham Park today. The Domesday Survey of 1086 recorded a village and church, supported by a hide of land at Bowdon, and that the county as a whole was comparatively poor and remote. A Roman road called Watling Street – part of which connected Deva (Chester) to Mamucium (Manchester) – followed a straight line between the two villages, providing access to other parts of the region.

Changes came when the Norman army, commanded by Hugh d'Avranches, marched westward along the Bollin Valley from Stockport and erected a motte and bailey, which later became a castle. This was at the point where Watling Street forded the River Bollin and is now called Castle Hill. From this point Hugh divided his troops, one contingent travelled down the Roman road and the other one went by a more westerly route, to take the city of Chester in a pincer movement, thus completing the conquest of England. For his success Hugh was awarded the Earldom of Chester and he, in turn, granted the Barony of Dunham, including the village of Bowdon, to one of his officers, Hamon de Massey in 1070, ousting Alweard and his family. Following these events, de Massey built himself a baronial hall, Dunham Massey, with a demesne which included the large Saxon deer park for hunting.

In order to impress the native population with the majesty of the church and the power of their rulers, the crude Saxon church was replaced with a new one, designed in accordance with the principles of Romanesque architecture, to become the parish church serving the estate. Improved administration replaced the former stagnant economy, enabling development in agriculture and local trade. This included the working of salt springs along the Bollin River so that in 1320, with an increased population, the church was restored and enlarged and a tower built. It was characterised by more delicate detailing than previously with simple but more elegant features, generally classified as Early English.

Later a clerestory was built over the nave and extensions carried out at the east end but, except for alterations to doors and windows, the church changed very little until the eighteenth century. The church drew its income from tithes; grain was taken and barns, such as the one still standing at Ashley Heath, were built for the purpose. In the twelfth century Hamon de Massey, the 3rd Baron, founded Birkenhead Priory and endowed it with land in Bowdon. This was followed by the 5th Baron granting the advowson of the church to the priory. Glebe land, on which the vicarage stood, provided support for the local church and the priest, but all the land (except for a small area of glebe on which the vicarage stood) was turned over to the Bishop of Chester by Henry VIII following the Reformation.

The barony was divided into manors, with manor houses or halls for the Lords of the Manor. An excellent example exists at Ashley Heath, which may originally have been Motley Hall. Robert de Massey granted land to Adam de Bowdon, a member of a local family of ancient rank, but retained the manorial rights for himself. Bowdon Hall, which Adam de Bowdon built, never strictly became a manor house.

The hamlet adjacent to the church consisted of simple thatched cottages that were supplied with water from various sources including 'The Springs' in Bow Green Lane, which were reputed to have medicinal qualities. Longhouses served as farmsteads in which provision was made for livestock, grain storage and living accommodation under a single roof. Larger dwellings provided more sophisticated houses for yeomen, similar to the one at Little Bollington. All the local buildings, with the exception of the church which was built of stone, were built in cruck timber-frame construction with thatched roofs using local materials and craftsmanship to best advantage.

During the same period, following a royal grant of the right to hold a market, the de Massey's created Altrincham, a free borough of burgesses with some degree of self-administration under baronial rule. Altrincham developed into a prosperous market town which the villages of Bowdon and Dunham relied upon for the sale of their agricultural produce.

The 1086 Domesday entry of Hamo de Massey's holdings. The translation reads, 'Hamo also holds Bowdon. Alfward held it; he was a free man, 1 hide paying tax Land for 2 ploughs, 2 Frenchmen have 1 plough. A priest and a church, to whom a half of this hide belongs. A mill which pays 16d. Value 3s; it was waste; and he found it so.'

Bowdon Church as it probably appeared in the twelfth century.

Bowdon Church from Church Brow, c. 1850.

Old Bowdon Church prior to rebuilding in 1860.

The tithe barn at Ashley Heath was used for the storage of grain that was collected as the local tithe.

This postcard of cottages, postmarked 1906, on Church Brow was inscribed with, 'Think I could live here for ever, Annie'.

The back of one of the cottages on Church Brow showing timber-frame construction.

OLD THATCHED COTTAGE, OLDFIELD BROW, ALTRINCHAM.

The longhouse at Oldfield Brow, c. 1925.

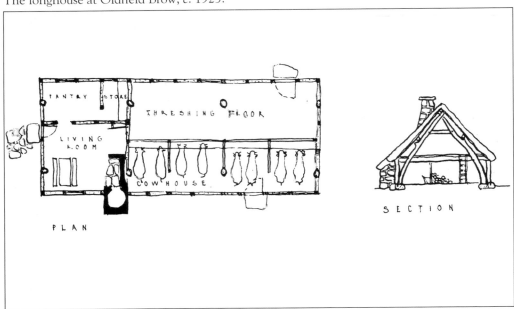

PANTRY STORE

THRESHING FLOOR

LIVING
ROOM

COW HOUSE

PLAN

SECTION

The plan and section views of the same longhouse. Originally a combined farmstead and farmhouse, it was used as three cottages before being converted to one farmhouse at a later date.

Timber-frame and cruck construction at the Oldfield Brow longhouse.

Medieval medicinal springs in Bow Green Road.

Old House, Ashley Heath.

A yeoman's house at Little Bollington (formerly Bollington), part of the Dunham Massey estate.

Two

The Booths

The estate passed from the de Massey family when, in 1453, Sir Robert Booth of Barton inherited it through the female line of his family. Around 1616, Sir George Booth rebuilt the old timber-framed Hall in brickwork, following the introduction of brick making into the district. Sir George's grandson, also Sir George and later 1st Lord Delamer, enlarged the house and added a new entrance with octagonal hunting towers at each end from which spectators could watch stag hunting in the park. In 1553 Edward Janny left Robert Vaudrey money to pay for a school to be founded in Bowdon. This became the Parish National School in the early nineteenth century.

During this period the rural economy continued to develop, along with the rest of the county, and the influence of the Booth family gained prominence both locally and nationally. In the troubled period of the seventeenth century, the Booths, who were independently minded, supported Parliament against the Royalists. They became disenchanted with Cromwell when he took on the powers of dictatorship and actively supported the restoration of the monarchy. The autocratic rule of James II made them disillusioned with the Stuarts and the 2nd Lord Delamer openly supported the Duke of Monmouth, entertaining him at Dunham Massey Hall. For his involvement in the Monmouth cause, Booth was arrested and brought to trial by his peers, before the notorious Lord Chancellor Jeffreys. Booth was acquitted of high treason as he was helped by the supportive evidence of his steward John Edmonds. Booth continued his opposition, however, until James was forced to abdicate, when he was selected to escort the former King to the coast and oversee his departure into exile. The new King William III rewarded Booth with the enhanced title of Earl of Warrington, but his political aspirations brought him to the very brink of bankruptcy.

On the death of the 1st Earl of Warrington in 1694, his son, George Booth, became the 2nd Earl and inherited a neglected estate and a Hall which he described as being 'so decayed as forced me to rebuild it, for it could not have lasted safe another generation'. After refusing to take any part in national affairs, he set about restoring both the estate and the Hall. Marriage in 1702 to Mary Oldbury, a wealthy heiress, provided George Booth with the means to undertake this tremendous task. Although they were totally incompatible and lived separate lives within the same house, the birth of a daughter in 1704 brought a beneficiary to his life's work restoring Dunham Massey.

New farmsteads and cottages were built, tenancies were organized on a viable basis that was advantageous to both landlord and tenant, and compulsory tree planting by farmers was introduced. John Edmonds remained in his post as a steward to the Earl, living in the rebuilt Bowdon Hall. He received national acclaim as an improver of agriculture: his achievements probably included planting tree nurseries at Headman's Covert and Pitstead Covert. Extensive drainage of the marshes north of Dunham Massey was undertaken and the salt springs along the Bollin were developed into a prosperous salt works and village at Dunham Woodhouses by Thomas Walton. Part of the large fortune he made was left to local charity and used for various purposes including the building of a village school at Little Heath and Bowdon Grammar School at Oldfield Brow. The grammar school took boarders and taught Greek and Latin. In 1766 a Cornishman, William Trenbath, was appointed as a revenue officer to oversee the payment of Salt Tax in the district, which had been widely evaded over a long period of time.

When his finances became sufficiently secure, George Booth replanted the deer park, for profit and ostentation purposes, in accordance with Dutch principles of landscape design. He also began the major task of rebuilding the Hall, which was to include a fine library, a vast silver collection and stabling for a large number of horses.

This picture of Dunham Massey Hall was painted in 1697. It was built to a design popular at the time with corner hunting towers.

The Booths were a very influential family both locally and nationally, who impoverished themselves through participation in politics. *Above left:* Sir George Booth. *Above right:* Sir George's grandson (also Sir George), the 1st Lord Delamer. *Right:* Henry Booth, 2nd Lord Delamer and 1st Earl of Warrington.

An early eighteenth-century painting of the deer park, Dunham Massey.

The lodge gates at Dunham Massey Hall were destroyed by enemy action in 1940 (see p. 118).

George Booth, the 2nd Earl of Warrington, and his daughter Mary, the Countess of Stamford, together restored the Hall and the estate following its decline in the seventeenth century.

Dunham Massey Hall, the parterre and the moat. The moat was decorative and had no defensive purpose as it could easily have been breached.

The blackamoor statue with coach houses that were built in 1721 behind.

The deer house in the park was built in 1740.

The orangery was used for cultivating oranges and exotic fruits.

Large stables accommodated the great number of horses required by the Booth family.

A sixteenth-century hunting scene.

The seventeenth-century watermill, which was powered for short periods by water from the moat, served Dunham Massey Hall and the estate by grinding corn, but was later used as a sawmill known locally as 'The Dunham Ripper'.

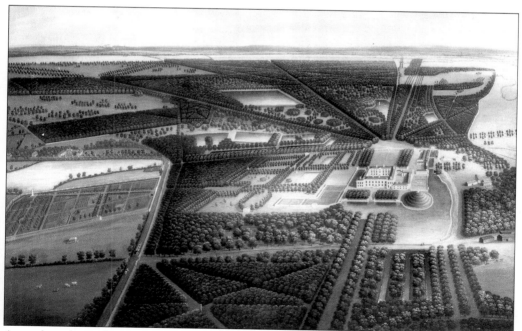

An early eighteenth-century view of the deer park, Hall and gardens.

This early eighteenth-century chapel at Hale Barns served the needs of local Nonconformists.

A cottage built in 1666, South Downs Road, Bowdon.

An early eighteenth-century house and cottages, Dunham Town. The 2nd Earl of Warrington provided a high standard of housing for his tenants.

Bowdon Hall in the nineteenth century.

The probable appearance of Bowdon Hall, *c.* 1700. Bowdon Hall was the home of John Edmonds, land improver and steward to the Earl. The inclusion of the cupola is based upon inconclusive structural evidence.

Three
The Stamfords

On his death in 1758 the 2nd Earl of Warrington bequeathed the whole estate to his daughter, Lady Mary Booth, who had married Harry, Lord Grey of Groby (later the 4th Earl of Stamford). It was she, and not her husband, who took over the management of the estate at Dunham Massey, maintaining the house and grounds and continuing the programme of tree planting and improvements.

The cutting of the canal through Dunham by the Duke of Bridgewater and improvements to the main Chester Road, when it became a turnpike thoroughfare, were very beneficial to developing industries. It was possible to transport coal from Worsley and move salt from the wharf constructed at Dunham. Improved links were made with Central Cheshire, the Potteries and Liverpool, and the village of Little Bollington was developed with the addition of weavers' cottages. This expansion reinforced the Countess' efforts to improve the economy and consequently the prosperity of Dunham and Bowdon, and it also accounted for the growth of industry in Altrincham.

The increase in population, which resulted from these developments, created overcrowding at the parish church in Bowdon. Galleries were built in the church to provide extra space, including a private gallery for the Earl and his family and St George's, a chapel of ease, was also built in Altrincham in 1799 to help relieve the problem.

The increased local affluence, however, brought an outbreak of criminal activity to the area in the form of highway robbery, mugging, burglary and murder. Many malefactors were caught and punished, including the notorious Thomas Brennan (known as 'Timperley Tom') whose body was hung from a gibbet on the main road after he had been hanged in Chester. It has been recorded that local residents were always armed when outside their homes.

Both the 5th and the 6th Earl travelled in Italy, while the former rebuilt the south front of the Hall in 1789 to a rather dreary and uninspired design. Neither of the earls were interested in politics, each preferring to focus his attention on the maintenance and improvement of the estates and on sporting activities. A large architecturally designed home farm was built adjacent to the park's main entrance, off Chester Road, in order to impress visitors. As well as its functions as a farm and to provide food for the Hall, it was also a centre for sporting activities. In the main yard, coach houses were built with arches and supported on columns, under which carriages could be parked. An elegant dovecote was built in the centre of the yard to house pigeons used in shooting competitions. An arcade held sophisticated cages for birds and was used for cock-fighting, while in the nearby coverts game birds were reared by the gamekeepers. A small mere was used for fishing competitions.

The flat land between the park and Chester Road was used for steeplechasing – including the Dunham Massey Stakes – and the hunt met regularly at the Hall. The stables were further enlarged to facilitate the increased number of horses required for these events as well as the racing fixtures at Knutsford. These activities, together with the attendant balls, were the main social events of the district.

Whitehouse Farm, Dunham Massey, a small eighteenth-century farmhouse.

Bollington Hall Farm, Park Lane, Little Bollington, which was rebuilt in 1770. Note the ladder window designed to reduce the window tax.

The eighteenth-century barn at Home Farm, which could be found adjacent to the park's main entrance, off Chester Road. Note the decorative use of air holes and the pitching eye used for loading sheaves of corn into the building.

Oldfield Farm was often visited by John Wesley who 'preached under a pear tree' there.

An eighteenth-century farmstead, West Bank Farm, Bow Green.

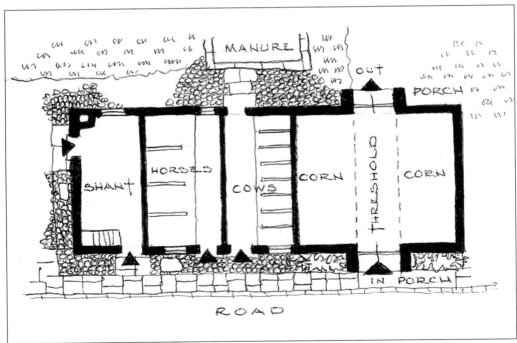

The plan of the West Bank farmstead. Note the threshing floor and the threshold and porches with splayed cheeks to control draught during the process.

Early nineteenth-century cottages and cattle pound, Bow Green.

Yew Tree Cottage and Whitfield Cottage, Bow Green, c. 1870. These cottages are examples of how early nineteenth-century housing improved locally following the agricultural revolution.

33

Norman's Place, Altrincham. These houses were built as one person's dwellings, not as family houses. They were provided with spacious living rooms and bedrooms decorated with fireplaces, cornices and detailing far beyond the standard available to middle class residents in the eighteenth century. Each had a small bedroom for a servant and, at one time, the houses may have been used by impoverished persons of rank.

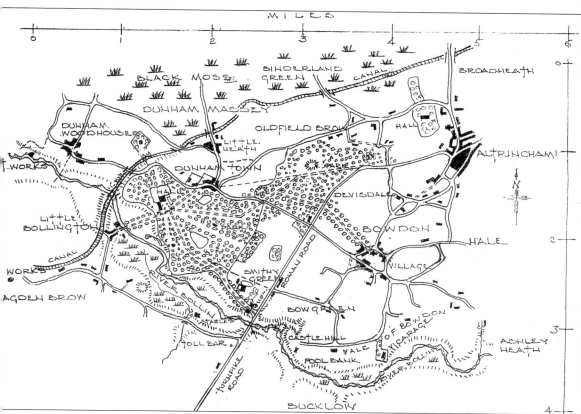

The building of the
Bridgewater Canal
and the introduction
of turnpike roads led
to an improvement in
transport. This
encouraged economic
development.

A drawing of a
tollgate from the
Bowdon area.

Eighteenth-century salt workers' cottages, Dunham Woodhouses.

Early cottages. Dunham Woodhouses developed into a thriving salt village in the eighteenth century, based upon the ancient salt springs on the banks of the River Bollin.

Manor Farm, Dunham Woodhouses. This was the home of Thomas Walton, a Salt Master who was responsible for the development of Dunham Woodhouses as a salt village.

The house of an official, 1752.

AN
ABRIDGEMENT
OF ALL THE
STATUTES
Now in FORCE,

Relating to the Duties on

SALT and HERRINGS,

Digested under the following Heads, viz.

ENGLISH SALT. | FISH and FISHERY.
FOREIGN SALT. | BEEF and PORK.
SALT made in Scotland. | SALT DUTIES in general.

To which is added, under the Head of

BEEF and PORK,

An ABSTRACT of the Laws that pro-
hibit the Importation of BEEF and
PORK from *Ireland*, and other Foreign
Parts.

LONDON:

Printed by *Thomas Baskett*, Printer to the King's
most Excellent Majesty; and by the Assigns of
Robert Baskett; for *J.* and *R. Tonson* in the
Strand. 1746.

A Salt Officer's manual. William Trenbath was appointed revenue officer to oversee payment of Salt Tax in 1766, having previously served in Northwich since 1761.

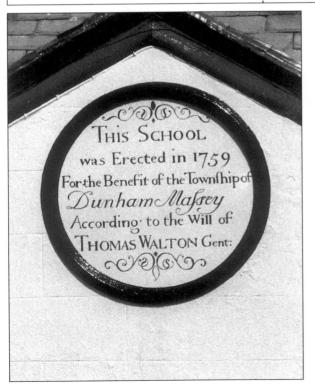

THIS SCHOOL
was Erected in 1759
For the Benefit of the Township of
Dunham Massey
According to the Will of
THOMAS WALTON Gent:

Plaque on the village school at Little Heath, Dunham Massey. The school was built through money left by Thomas Walton for local charitable use.

Bowdon Grammar School, Oldfield Brow, *c.* 1925.

The village school, Little Heath. Both the grammar school and the village school were built as a result of the charitable legacy provided in Thomas Walton's will.

Former salt works, adjacent to the Bridgewater Canal, Agden, in 1998.

The canal in 1999.

An early nineteenth-century toll-house in Chester Road, Bucklow Hill, *c.* 1890.

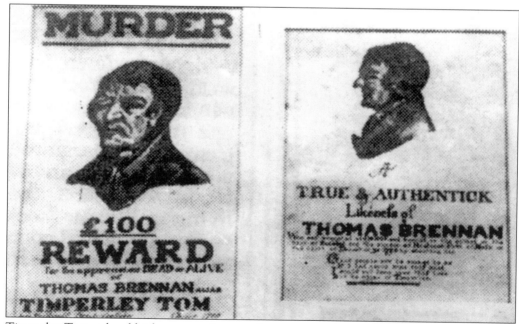

Timperley Tom, a local highwayman. Improved transport and economic development gave rise to criminal activities such as murder and highway robbery. Tom was hanged at Chester and his body displayed locally.

Village street, Little Bollington.

Weavers' cottages and 'Swan With Two Nicks', Little Bollington, developed through the weaving industry, following the cutting of the canal. The village was destroyed by enemy action in 1940 (see p. 118).

The dovecote, Home Farm, Dunham Hall. Home Farm was used as a centre for sporting activities by the local gentry as well as being a provider of food for the Hall. The dovecote housed birds used in shooting competitions.

Cages for cockfighting birds at Home Farm.

Until recently the fishing lake at Home Farm was used for competitions.

An early nineteenth-century print of a fishing competition.

Above: The head gamekeeper's house, Bow Green.
The Stamfords were great sportsmen who entertained
their guests lavishly. *Right:* The 6th Earl of Stamford.

Dunham Town and ancient tree, *c.* 1890.

The eighteenth-century Axe and Cleaver Inn, Dunham Town, *c.* 1890.

A local omnibus which served the area in the early nineteenth century.

An early nineteenth-century billhead. Note the omnibus.

An early nineteenth-century print of an omnibus travelling along Burying Lane (now The Firs) towards the old church.

Griffin Inn and Bowdon Church in the early nineteenth century. Bear-baiting was regularly practised at the tree in front of the church.

A late eighteenth-century print of the interior of old Bowdon Church.

The staircase to the Stamford Gallery was originally in the old Bowdon Church. It was moved here to its present position, Downs Cottage, Woodville Road, when the church was rebuilt (see p. 51).

The twin house attached to this building was the premises of William Wood who campaigned with Lord Shaftesbury for legislation to prohibit the use of boys as chimney sweeps.

Cottage Orné houses, Stamford Road, Bowdon. The Cottage Orné style was a remnant of the Picturesque movement prevalent in late eighteenth-century Europe.

Downs Cottage, Woodville Road, Bowdon.

Bowdon Downs Congregational Church, Bowdon. The church was built to serve the growing Nonconformist population and used an elegant Strawberry Hill-type design.

2-2-2T engine *Flora* was built by Sharp Brothers & Co., Manchester, and used on the Manchester South Junction and Altrincham Railway in the 1850s.

This is the first ticket issued on 20 July 1849. Issac Warburton ran from his home in Langham Road, Bowdon, to the station determined to buy the first ticket. It was eventually given to Altrincham Library and was on display for many years.

Cabs outside the former Bowdon station. The station was opened in 1849 and closed in 1881.

Four

The Cottontots

Until the middle of the nineteenth century local land was mainly held by the Stamfords, the Assheton Smiths and the Church. It was distributed widely in small parcels over the district, until the parties concerned agreed to consolidate their holdings on a give and take basis. Thomas Assheton Smith, who did not have any local ties, decided to sell his land in Bowdon. The land that he owned on the southern downs was bought for residential development as it had potential for high-class housing, due to its position and magnificent views over the Chester Plain.

The appeal of the area was further enhanced by the introduction of improved passenger transport: a horse-drawn omnibus service and passenger packet barges on the canal, which were drawn by fast horses that were frequently changed. The development was given the romantic name of Rose Hill. Elizabeth Gaskell regularly came to stay at Moss Farm, with her children, for the good of their health. She wrote an interesting account of children being brought in barges for days out at Whitsun, which contrasted the beauty of Dunham Park with the pollution of Manchester where they lived.

The Rose Hill project was fairly small scale, consisting of villas, semi-detached houses and terraces. These were mainly Georgian and Regency in character, with a few that followed Gothic Revival or Cottage Orné trends. Albert Square, the next development, was built within walking distance of the new Bowdon station. It was constructed at the bottom of the Downs following the construction of the railway in 1849, which linked Altrincham with the industrial belt north of the Mersey. Both the Downs and Burying Lane (renamed The Firs) were also attracting housebuilders at this time. The first large house built was High Lawn, an Italianate mansion on Rose Hill, to accommodate William Neild, a calico printer, and his family.

Until the death of the 6th Earl the Stamford Estate resolutely refused to release land for housing but, after his death in 1845 at the age of eighty, the policy was changed. Disagreement between the new 7th Earl and local Bowdon residents caused him to live on his other estates, except for visits for hunting and shooting parties. From 1883 to 1891 the Hall was rented to tenants and from 1891 until 1906 it was left unoccupied.

Georgian-style houses, South Road, Rose Hill, Bowdon.

In 1857 the young Earl showed considerable business acumen when he proposed a grand residential scheme adjacent to his park and centred on a new church to be named after his sister Margaret. The church was built in Gothic style with a tall spire and magnificent detailing. It was admired as the finest architectural design in the area with the exception of the non-conformist Higher Downs Church built a few years previously. St Margaret's was consecrated in 1855 and became the parish church of Dunham Massey.

An excellent overall plan allowed the road leading from the church to Bowdon village (renamed St Margaret's Road) to be realigned as a straight, wide, tree-lined thoroughfare with similar roads leading off it. Covenants in the deeds ensured that the new houses conformed in size, value, status and appearance, as required by the Earl. During the next twenty years this resulted in the erection of palatial mansions in large landscaped gardens, and the introduction of white brick, which the Earl favoured and for which the district became noted.

The surveyor to the estate, Maxwell Roscoe, was mainly responsible for the planning and supervision of the venture, which encouraged very rich families to settle in the area. In particular, these were families of the industrial and commercial entrepreneurs from the north who wished to escape to a more salubrious environment. The most noteworthy residence in the scheme was Denzell, a large mansion set in ten acres of landscaped garden, built for Robert Scott to the designs of the architects Clegg & Knowles and sumptuously finished, in mainly Flemish style, with a vinery, and peach and orchid houses. The 1881 census records that Scott and his wife employed nine servants: a butler, an under butler, a cook, a housemaid, two domestic servants, a head gardener, a coachman and a groom.

From census returns it would appear that most of the new residents, and many of their servants, came from all parts of Britain, with a few even arriving from Europe. They were drawn to the north by

54

the growing economy that resulted from the expansion of the cotton industry and ancillary trades to produce a unique local cosmopolitan society in Bowdon. It was claimed that more millionaires lived on Green Walk, Bowdon, than Park Lane in London.

In 1860 the parishioners rebuilt and enlarged the parish church in Bowdon to the designs of the architect W.H. Brakspear. In 1880 the Methodists built a large domed chapel, a short distance away, that was also designed by Brakspear. He also designed a new vicarage for the church to replace the previous one which had been sold as a private residence and renamed Bowdon Priory.

The Stamford Arms was rebuilt opposite the church and next to the Green Dragon, which is now renamed the Griffin Inn. They served the parishioners, with the former entertaining the employers and the latter serving the employees. In 1867 St John's Church was founded to meet the spiritual needs of the poor members of the community who, it was said, were an embarrassment to the rich members of St Margaret's congregation.

Mindful of the social needs of the non-resident employees, Bowdon Vale, an ancillary village on the lower reaches of the hill, was built to provide for their requirements. These included houses, shops, allotments, community clubs and facilities for good works: it was often called 'Soapy Town' due to the number of laundresses who plied their trade there. The Parish National School was rebuilt and Bible classes, Boys and Girls Clubs and Adult Education facilities were formed, together with Penny Savings Banks and a Ladies Committee, to oversee the moral welfare of young women. These provisions were often resented as they were considered patronising and paternalistic, especially by the tenants and workers on the Stamford Estate who could afford to show an independent spirit against the Cottontots.

In spite of their concern for the welfare of their domestic employees, the Cottontots showed scant interest in the well-being of their labour force. In a world orientated around toil, mechanization and

Gothic revival-style houses, Langham Road, Rose Hill.

Early Victorian houses, Rose Hill.

profit there were some rich philanthropists; Francis Crossley a brilliant and wealthy engineer was perhaps unique in leaving, Fairlie, his house in Bowdon, to live among the poor of Ancoats and attend to their welfare. William Wood also had a social conscience, working hard to reform the laws regarding child labour and, in particular, the plight of young chimney sweeps.

The introduction of local threshing machines in 1847 made traditional threshing barns redundant, replaced by open-sided cathedral barns. A new watermill was built on the Bollin at Little Bollington to grind corn for dairy cattle, but many farmers concentrated on growing hay to feed the new residents' horses, rather than corn. Some farmers, such as the Chesters in Bow Green, completely changed from general farming to market gardening in order to meet the increased demand for fruit and vegetables. They also opened dairies and provided delivery services, which proved to be very lucrative. The increased prosperity in local agriculture led to the formation of an Agricultural Society and the holding of the Altrincham Agricultural Show annually. Taking place on former common land called the Devisdale, the show later developed into the largest one-day event of its type in the country as well as a great local occasion.

During this period the local market town of Altrincham expanded, with the introduction of industry at Broadheath, to include extended shopping facilities to be patronised by the people from Bowdon and Dunham Massey. A few shops, named The Polygon, were built in Bowdon village, including a chemist, a grocer and a photographer to meet the immediate needs of the neighbourhood. New houses in Altrincham spread to the boundary of Bowdon and Dunham Massey, resulting in Bowdon virtually becoming a suburb of Altrincham. It retained its independence, however, and was made an Urban District in 1894.

The area's reputation for having a clean and healthy environment may account for the opening of a number of nursing homes, a sanatorium and the Bowdon Hydro, which provided residential spar treatment for ailing visitors. The clean air also made it an excellent point for observing stars and many of the new residents incorporated observatories and telescopes into their properties. Consideration was given to rebuilding the Royal Observatory in Bowdon when it moved from Greenwich.

Many of Rose Hill's early residents started boarding schools in their houses, ranging from small preparatory schools to ladies' seminaries. These took advantage of the fact that many parents were prepared to pay for their children to be educated in a very healthy environment. J.M.D. Meiklejohn, the eminent educationalist, founded the Rose Hill School for Boys, which was taken over and expanded by Alfred J. Pearce BA, Miss Gregson started Highbury School, George Schelling ran a school which provided Continental-type education and the Misses Lang brought their school to Bowdon and named it Culcheth Hall School for Girls. In 1870 Bowdon College was founded by Theophilis D. Hall MA as a boarding school to replace Bowdon Grammar School, which was converted into a private residence. These new schools, together with those in Altrincham, provided education for all sections of the community.

During the early stages of the development of Bowdon, new residents began socialising. Many held soirées, inviting friends and neighbours, often to meet distinguished guests. As a result of these parties dining clubs were formed, and these increased in number, size and variety during the rest of the century. The first of these, the Roundabout Club, was founded in the early 1860s by Alexander Ireland, a newspaper proprietor, in association with Mr Meiklejohn and Horatio Micholls, an influential Jewish merchant. The club consisted of twelve gentlemen who met monthly for dinner at each member's house. They met famous visitors or discussed topics of interest in an atmosphere of geniality and freedom of expression. John Bright and Charles Hallé often numbered among the honoured guests.

Rose Hill was the first area to be developed when Thomas Assheton Smith sold on land in the south-facing Bowdon Downs.

The Firs, Bowdon, was formerly Burying Lane.

Alexander Ireland, who had a library of 20,000 books, lived at Inglewood, St Margaret's Road. He was a friend of Thomas Carlyle, Nathaniel Hawthorne and Emerson, an acquaintance of Wordsworth, Lamb, Leigh Hunt, De Quincey and Elizabeth Gaskell, and he also gave his personal support to Louis Kossuth the Hungarian nationalist and Count Saffi, the Italian patriot. Some of these figures visited him in Bowdon.

Between 1879 and 1880 Theophilis D. Hall formed the more specific Bowdon Literary and Science Club. Members met in each others houses until the membership became too big for this to be practical and they had to meet in the Parish Hall. The president, who was elected from the members in turn, included Dr Arthur Ransome FRS (cousin of the author of the same name), Canon Wainwright, Dr Males, Professor Hull and E.J. Sidebotham. The guest speakers included figures such as Matthew Arnold and Sir Oliver Lodge. Membership was restricted to men but it was extended to include women on suitable occasions.

The 60 Club was formed later in the nineteenth century to provide talks and entertainment for both sexes. Meetings were held regularly in members' houses and restricted to sixty as many of the houses could not accommodate more than that number of guests. The number increased when meetings were held in the newly built Assembly Rooms. John Mills, a successful banker, economist and amateur musician attended musical soirées at the home of Mrs Louis Behrens in Green Walk. The club also heard performances by members of 'Hallé's Band' and Alexander Ireland held musical evenings at his home where talented amateur musicians entertained each other. It was as a result of these performances that Alexander's son, Dr John Ireland, who was to become a distinguished composer, first took an interest in music.

In 1901 Hans Richter, Wagner's musical secretary and the former conductor of the Vienna Philharmonic Orchestra, came to live in The Firs. During his term of office as conductor of the Hallé

Orchestra, he entertained many of the leading musicians and composers of the day. These included Bartók, who was very impressed with Dunham Massey and Bowdon: he wrote to his mother in Budapest extolling their beauty. Adolf Brodsky, the Russian violinist and great friend of Tchaikovsky, was appointed leader of the Hallé and Principal of the Royal Manchester College of Music. In 1905 he took up residence at 3 Laurel Bank, where he also entertained leading musicians and their families including the wife of the Norwegian composer Grieg. Many eminent musicians also performed at the Bowdon Chamber Concerts given the Assembly Rooms from 1908 to 1934, including Myra Hess, Elisabeth Schumann, Schnabel, Moseiwitsch and John Ireland.

Authors who lived in Bowdon included Juliana Ewing and Alison Uttley. Howard Spring was a frequent visitor who knew the area well. He used it as a location for many of his tales, graphically describing social life at that time. Harrison Ainsworth, who had relatives locally, also used Dunham Massey as a location for many of his plots.

The visual arts were represented by Randolph Caldecott, Byron Cooper, Gladys Vasey and Helen Allingham, whose father was a local doctor. Many of the early residents, such as James Mudd and Joseph Sidebotham who took local photographs from 1852, were pioneering photographers. The famous Frith's Postcard Company was founded locally. T.A. Coward, the internationally recognised ornithologist and local historian, was born here and lived in the area all his life.

Sports clubs provided facilities for bowling, hockey, football and cricket in Bowdon, Bowdon Vale and Dunham Massey to serve the whole of the community. An exclusive golf club for men, which was built at Dunham Town, closed down during the Second World War. Cycling became a very popular pastime for both men and women and at weekends cycling clubs from the north often passed through the district on their way to North Wales.

Albert Square in Bowdon was developed with medium sized houses following the building of the railway in 1849. Note the roof and spire of the Presbyterian church.

High Lawn, Rose Hill, was built for William Neild, a calico printer. He was the second Mayor of Manchester.

A nineteenth-century family playing croquet at The Beeches, Higher Downs. It was later renamed St Ann's Hospital, after the wife of the last owner of the house, as a stipulation of the sale. Croquet was introduced in the mid-1860s and it soon became popular as a sport in which women could participate. Note Bowdon Downs Church in the background.

St Margaret's Church, *c.* 1890. This elegant church was built by the 7th Earl and named after his sister. It was later designated the parish church of Dunham Massey. The spire became unsafe and was dismantled in the 1920s, and an extension was built on the west end.

Denzell, Green Walk, from the croquet lawn. Denzell, the largest and most opulent of the great mansions, was built in Bowdon to the design of the architects, Clegg & Knowles, for Robert Scott, his wife and their nine servants.

The pond in the garden at Denzell was formerly a fountain.

An architect's perspective of Denzell.

An architect's perspective of the Gate Lodge to Denzell on Dunham Road. The buildings were designed in an idiosyncratic Flemish style popular at the time. Howard Spring used Denzell as a location for one of his novels, giving a graphic description of Bowdon life in the nineteenth century.

Domestic staff at Denzell in the time of Samuel Lamb, the owner from 1905. The staff were privileged, being well housed, fed and clothed, compared with the underprivileged workers in industrial areas.

A Bowdon family travelling in their landau.

Spring cleaning at the Priory
involved beating carpets.

The housekeeper and
housemaids at Dunham
House, which was built by
Walter Joynson in 1899.

An architect's perspective of Erlesdene, Green Walk, Bowdon, which was designed in a pseudo-Elizabethan style popular at the time.

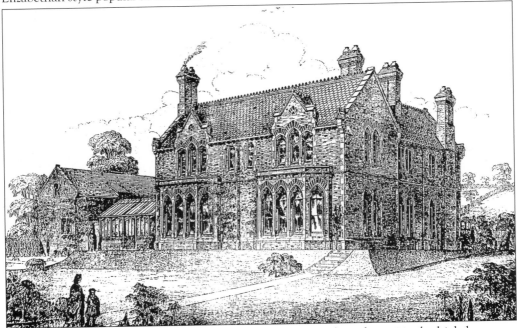

The New Vicarage in Park Road, Bowdon, was built to replace the original which became a private residence and was renamed The Priory.

Green Walk, Bowdon, was formerly part of a private drive connecting Dunham Massey Hall with the parish church.

Helene Witte (right) with her parents from Germany in the drawing room at Dunham Rise, *c.* 1902. Helene Opitz from Stuttgart married Julius Witte of Manchester and moved to Dunham Rise in 1887. Julius Witte was a partner in the firm of Beatty-Altgelt, shipping merchants. After his death in 1907 Helene, despite never having worked previously, had to take his place. In 1914 she was considered an enemy as she had not become naturalised and still had a German passport. Her capital was confiscated and the name of the firm was changed to Witte & Ddyckhoff. Helene's son and daughter lived at Dunham Rise until the 1960s when the son died and the house was sold as development land.

An architect's perspective of the new parish church, *c.* 1859.

The parish church, after its completion in 1860, with the Griffin Inn and the cab rank. The new church replaced its medieval predecessor, which was in need of repair and too small for the increasing population.

The Polygon, Bowdon, *c.* 1910. The Polygon was built to provide shopping facilities in developing Bowdon. The photographer's daylight studio, which was typical of the period, can be seen today. John Thompson practised from around 1907 to 1916 and was one of at least five photographers who occupied the studio from 1883 to 1921. The chemist's shop was owned by Robert Tootill, who had other shops in Altrincham, Hale and Sale. After the First World War he sold out to Boots.

Reverend James Thomas Law was the vicar of Bowdon from 1815 to 1826.

The Stamford Arms, Bowdon, was rebuilt to serve more affluent residents. The adjoining Griffin served the less wealthy.

The Pavilion was added onto the Stamford Arms for social receptions.

The Parish National School, Richmond Road.

Pupils of the National School, c. 1900.

A horticultural lesson at the National School, The Firs, *c.* 1900.

An early private school in Langham Road, Bowdon. Private houses in Bowdon were often used as small schools or as 'Dame' Schools.

Bowdon College was a boarding school for boys which replaced Bowdon Grammar School in the early 1870s. It was demolished in 1998 and replaced by the College Flats that were built on the site in 1999.

Culcheth Hall School for Girls. Private schools in early nineteenth-century Bowdon provided healthy living conditions for pupils from areas polluted by industry.

Highbury School in West Road, Bowdon, a purpose-built school for older girls that was established in the 1870s.

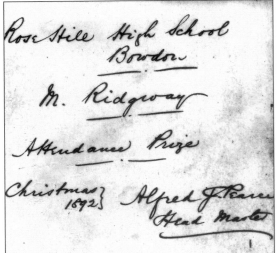

THE HIGH SCHOOL,
ROSE HILL,
BOWDON.

Left: The certificate of a prize given at the High School, Rose Hill, to M. Ridgway whose grandson, Canon Maurice Ridgway, was later appointed vicar of Bowdon. *Right:* The High School at Rose Hill.

The Wesleyan Methodist church, Bowdon, was built to the design of the architect W.H. Brakspear and opened in 1880. In the 1960s the church, which seated 300, became too costly to maintain and the final service was held on 21 August 1966.

St John's Church, St John's Road, c. 1865. Designed by the architect Medland Taylor, it was built to serve the poor members of the community and to provide a chapel of ease to St Margaret's. St John's was opened by Lord Stamford on 14 December 1866.

Directors of the old Literary Institute. Back row, left to right: Mr Smith, Mr Newton, Capt. Binney, Mr D. Morrison, Mr Fairhurst. Middle row: Mr Syers, Mr Clegg, Mr J.W. Byrom. Front row: Mr Balshaw, Mr Jas Drinkwater, Mr Meadows.

Francis Crossley was an engineer who left his comfortable home in Bowdon to live in the slums of Manchester, where he catered for the needs of the underprivileged at the Star Hall, Ancoats.

The Bowdon Hydro. The clean air attracted patients suffering from respiratory problems. The new Hydro provided spa treatment for these patients and those suffering from other ailments.

Langham Road. A typical Victorian scene in Bowdon, *c.* 1890.

Juliana Horatia Ewing (1841-1885) was a popular Victorian writer of numerous children's stories. She was admired by many contemporaries including Queen Victoria, Tennyson and Rudyard Kipling and was read by Arthur Ransome, the author of *Swallows and Amazons*, when he was a boy. The name 'Brownies', chosen by the Baden-Powells for junior Girl Guides, was suggested by the title of one of her stories.

Downs Villa, 14 Higher Downs, where Mrs Ewing and her husband, who was in the army, lived from 1877 to 1878. Her residence there is commemorated by a plaque.

Higher Downs can boast a second writer for children in Alison Uttley (1884-1976), who lived at Downs House. She is well known for her *Little Grey Rabbit* books, the first of which was written there, as were two of her other books, drawing on her Derbyshire childhood, *The Country Child* and *A Traveller in Time*.

Downs House, 13 Higher Downs, where Alison Uttley lived from 1924 to 1937. Her residence is commemorated by a plaque.

Dr Hans Richter.

Hans Richter (1843-1916), the great European conductor, was born in Hungary and studied in Vienna. He was a close associate of Wagner and was conductor of the Vienna Philharmonic Orchestra from 1880 until 1890. He conducted first performances of the *Enigma Variations*, *The Dream of Gerontius* and his first symphony, which Elgar dedicated to him with the words, 'True artist and true friend'.

Dr Richter's house, 27 The Firs, where he lived and entertained famous musicians from 1901 to 1911. The plaque on the house was unveiled by Lady Barbirolli, the widow of Sir John Barbirolli, conductor of the Hallé Orchestra between 1943 and 1970.

John Ireland (1879-1962) was a distinguished composer, especially for the piano and the voice. Born at Inglewood, St Margaret's Road, he was the son of Alexander Ireland (1810-94), publisher-manager of the advanced liberal newspaper the *Manchester Examiner and Times*, and a key figure in Manchester's cultural and political life. Both of John Ireland's parents were literary and well acquainted with famous authors such as Leigh Hunt, Emerson and Carlyle. Their home was a literary, artistic and musical centre in Bowdon, where the young John met Sir Charles Hallé. The family's fortunes waned in his father's last years when his paper succumbed to competition from the *Manchester Guardian*, but John Ireland had already gone to the Royal College of Music in London in 1893.

Inglewood in St Margaret's Road, Bowdon, was built by Alexander Ireland in 1870 after his second marriage in 1866. It was an imposing, detached house, in contrast to his more modest, Georgian-style house in Stamford Road.

Dr Adolph Brodsky (1851-1929) and his wife Anna in the garden of their Bowdon home. Brodsky, the world-famous Russian-born violinist, gave the first performance of Tchaikovsky's Violin Concerto under Richter in Vienna. He was appointed leader of the Hallé Orchestra in 1895 by Sir Charles Hallé and in the same year succeeded him as Principal of the Royal Manchester College of Music. His distinguished Brodsky Quartet was the dedicatee of Elgar's only string quartet. He had a wide circle of friends among great composers and musicians: Edvard Grieg's wife is known to have stayed. Thomas Pitfield, a nonagenarian resident in Bowdon, has vivid recollections of Brodsky from his own student days at the Royal Manchester College of Music.

Adolph Brodsky lived at 3 Laurel Mount, East Downs Road, from 1903 to 1929. His wife Anna, also of Russian origin, published nostalgic pieces on her native land as well as writing on Bowdon. 'At Home in England' is a charming description of a homecoming to their house in 1925. A plaque commemorating Brodsky's residence can be seen at the corner of the house.

The Bowdon Cricket, Hockey and Squash Club pavilion was built in 1874 on land bought by Miss H. Bickham of Gorsefield, Green Walk. The club was founded as Bowdon Cricket Club in 1856 by a group who practised on a piece of waste land on Rose Hill, later the site of the Wesleyan Chapel, South Road. After a period in Stamford Road a move was made around 1865 to the present site in South Downs Road. In 1888 the Bowdon Cricket and Hockey Club was formed and the squash section was added in 1969.

Bowdon Cricket Club First XI from 1937. Back row, left to right: F. Boland (umpire), K.A. Quas-Cohen, R.G. Shaw, W.H. Booth, W. Hanbridge, A.G. Gilbody, D.N. Walton, W. Sutcliffe (scorer). Front row: J.D. Worthington, G.F. Dugdale, G.K. Eaves (captain), J.A. Gilbody, G.P. Shaw.

The Bowdon Vale cricket team.

The Bowdon Vale football team, at the top of Priory Street. The team played in the Altrincham and District League. Members of the team are wearing white shirts. Back row, left to right: A. Hassell, H. Hall (goalkeeper), J. Essex. Middle row: F. Cain (captain), H. Hadfield, H. Smith, W. Pemberton. Front row: G. Giles, G. Bailey, P. Dean, H. Drinkwater, B. Smith. Wearing darker clothing, the staff on the left are: F. Ward (trainer), G.W. Clarke (secretary and treasurer), B. Dean. On the right: A. Spilsbury, L. Walker (groundsman), J. Burgess, P. Spilsbury.

A cycling event at Bowdon Cricket Club, *c.* 1900. South Downs Road runs along the end of the field.

Cyclists meet at the old barn at the junction of Bow Green Road and Langham Road. The barn was demolished around 1958.

Allotments in Bowdon Vale, *c.* 1950.

Village clubhouse, Bowdon Vale. Bowdon Vale was built on the lower reaches of Bowdon to provide housing and welfare facilities for the non-resident domestic staff of the residential area of the district.

Vicarage Lane, Bowdon Vale, *c.* 1905. Shops from left centre: Joseph Chester, greengrocer (see p. 89); William Fletcher, the butcher's with a carcass outside; William Fletcher, butcher; John Ackerley, grocer; Mrs Agnes Smith, a beer retailer with the sign advertising Groves & Whitnall's Ales. The shop on the right is possibly John Ackerley's second establishment.

A village policeman with the Gaddum children outside Primrose Cottages. Note the policeman's 'Shako' hat.

Sydney Spilsbury (left) and his brother Arthur delivering coal between Nos 12 and 14 Eaton Road, Bowdon Vale, *c.* 1910. The brothers worked for their father, a farmer with a milk and coal round and a haulage business.

Tenants of Primrose Cottages.

The Chester family at West Bank Farm, Bow Green.

Like many other local farmers, the Chesters moved from general farming to more lucrative activities such as market gardening and dairying, following residential development.

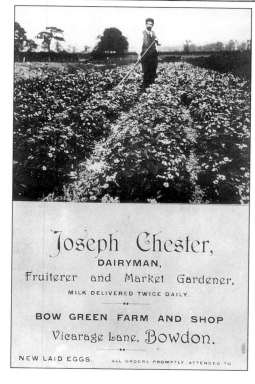

Joseph Chester,
DAIRYMAN,
Fruiterer and Market Gardener,
MILK DELIVERED TWICE DAILY.

BOW GREEN FARM AND SHOP
Vicarage Lane. Bowdon.

NEW LAID EGGS.   ALL ORDERS PROMPTLY ATTENDED TO.

Judging at the Altrincham Agricultural Show.

The Grand Parade at the Agricultural Show. The Altrincham Agricultural Show was held annually on the Devisdale, Bowdon. It was the largest one-day show in the country and one of the area's main events for the year. The Altrincham Agricultural Society formed in 1861. The first shows were held near the Swan Inn, later near Groby Road and then Devisdale from 1896 until it closed in 1966.

Village shop and post office, Dunham Town, *c.* 1890.

St Mark's Church, Dunham Town.

A group of houses at the corner of Vicarage Lane and Langham Road.

Due to Ruskin's influence, these houses were built in the form of an Italian villa with details taken from buildings in North Italy, such as those on Isola Dei Pescatori. The belvedere was demolished.

Five

The Return of the Stamfords

In 1906 the 9th Earl of Stamford returned to Dunham Massey and made it the permanent family home. Vast works of modernisation and redecoration were undertaken at the Hall including reconstruction of the south elevation, which was to have been built in the then popular Lutyens 'Wrennaisance' style (similar to the seventeenth-century Uppark, a famous stately home in Sussex owned by the National Trust). Unfortunately the architect J. Compton Hall carried out an idiosyncratic treatment of the entrance door, based on Sudbury Hall in Derbyshire, which the Earl considered very vulgar. He dismissed the architect, who agreed that it was a failure and would cause embarrassing derision for the family. Wartime restrictions prevented the Stamfords making any changes. The return of the Stamfords was celebrated with a great garden party held in the grounds of the Hall, attended by local residents and dignitaries. The Earl died in 1910 after only four years of residence, leaving the dowager Countess to manage the estate on behalf of their thirteen-year-old son, the former Viscount Groby, who became the 10th Earl. On coming of age he devoted much of his time to preserving and enhancing the estate.

In 1896 the first motor car was registered in Bowdon and soon afterwards Henry Royce used Chester Road and Bowdon Hill to test new models of Rolls Royce prior to going into production. It was a considerable time, however, before cars supplanted horses.

The flamboyant high-Victorian architecture of Bowdon went out of favour at the turn of the century and was replaced by the Arts and Crafts movement. A very fine example of the latter is Athelney in South Downs Road, together with a garden of the period, although Ruskin's Italian influence could be seen at an earlier period. Frank Dunkerley, a local wealthy dilettante architect, pupil of Voysey and Vice President of the Royal Institute of British Architects, designed several noteworthy buildings including the Bowdon Assembly Rooms. F.H. Brazier designed Lutyens-style houses in Bow Green Road as well as Windy Ridge on Church Brow, which later became the vicarage. At this time newly married couples showed preference for the more attractive and manageable houses in neighbouring Hale rather than the large mansions of Bowdon.

Rebuilt front elevation, Dunham Massey Hall. The Earl was displeased with the use of columns at the entrance and dismissed his architect who agreed that they were a mistake.

Around 1910 a new fee-paying school, the High School for Girls, was opened, with Miss Howes Smith, a former tutor to the Princess Royal, as headmistress. This was followed by the opening of a High School for Boys, with Mr Saville Laver as headmaster. Both schools soon gained very high academic success and gave priority to the development of individual character. Extra-curricular activities were designed to further that end, including an annual summer camp for pupils of the boys' school.

With the outbreak of war in 1914, the Earl of Stamford (when he attained military age) joined the army as aide-de-camp to General Lloyd. The Hall became a hospital where his sister, Lady Jane Grey, served as a nurse. Men from the district joined the forces, mainly the Cheshire Regiment, and the Cheshire yeomen drilled on the Devisdale. Many of the large houses were used as convalescent homes and events were organized to raise money for the war effort. Arthur Howorth, a local councillor, accepted a ministerial post in the wartime government for which he received a baronetcy.

A large prisoner-of-war camp was built at Sinderland Green, which was converted into an RAF munition depot after the war. German prisoners were made to undertake road building and land reclamation on Black Moss and Carrington Moss, and great animosity was shown towards them. The exception was the Reverend Hewlett-Johnson, vicar of St Margaret's and later the 'Red Dean' of Canterbury, who enraged local jingoists by trying to help them.

On one occasion a Zeppelin circled over Bowdon, confused by the two churches, before flying away to drop bombs on a slagheap in Bolton. Ex-servicemen, on their return from National Service, formed local branches of the British Legion and paraded every year at the newly erected Cenotaph, outside St Margaret's Church, to remember their fallen comrades. However, the whole experience of war left many of them disillusioned with the establishment and a changed attitude towards formerly respected institutions. The Earl, maintaining the radical traditions of his family, supported the Labour Party, became a great friend of Ramsay MacDonald and his family, and had involvement with the League of Nations. He provided sanctuary at the Hall to Haile Selassie, the Emperor of Ethiopia, during his exile in Britain. He also became an enthusiastic member of the Boy Scout movement, encouraging the formation of local scout troops and organizing gatherings in his park that were attended by Lord Baden-Powell. The 3rd Altrincham Troop, one of the largest in the country, built a large wooden Canadian-style headquarters, to the design of Brazier, at the High School for Boys.

The visit of Mary, the Princess Royal, to the High School for Girls to meet her friend and tutor, Miss Howes Smith, was an occasion for local celebration. The marriage of Ronald Gow, a former pupil and later a teacher at the High School for Boys, to Wendy Hiller, the award-winning actress, was also a time for festivity. Gow had become famous for producing educational films and later became a very successful dramatist and playwright. In 1936 Bowdon College closed down, mainly due to the success of the boys' High School, which was renamed Altrincham Grammar School. The house part of Bowdon College was converted into flats and the schoolrooms were used by the newly created Altrincham Preparatory School.

The use of horse-drawn transport rapidly declined and was succeeded by motor vehicles. The Automobile Association manned Chester Road with repair services and patrolmen on point duty.

William Grey, 9th Earl of Stamford, in a Spy cartoon in *Vanity Fair*.

The Earl and Countess with their children, Viscount Groby and Lady Jane Grey, at a garden party at Dunham Massey Hall to celebrate the return of the family in 1906.

Some local men took an interest in aeroplanes: John F. Leeming landed his plane on Chester Road to refuel with petrol from a newly opened petrol station and Harry Killick, who was a colourful local character and racing driver, built small planes called Flying Fleas in his workshop.

The failure of the cotton industry, succeeded by the world depression in the 1920s, severely affected the people of Bowdon. Many of the families moved south and those who stayed were forced to economise by reducing the size of their staff. Now seventy years old and out of date, most of the houses were in urgent need of repair and had overgrown gardens. In some cases mansions such as Erlesdene were left vacant in the charge of caretakers. This gave the area an air of great decrepitude. Sir Henry Veno, a patent medicine manufacturer, is thought to have taken his life in his garden due to financial losses and most of the local workers were reduced to part-time employment.

The cinema became the chief source of entertainment. The Altrincham Hippodrome was converted from a music hall into a cinema and two new ones, the Altrincham Picture Theatre and the Regal were built. Bowdon was served by the new Hale Cinema House which provided an orchestra and a small restaurant with page boys and a commissionaire in attendance.

Agriculture suffered badly from cheap foreign imports and the standard of husbandry deteriorated in spite of attempts by local landowners to assist the farmers. The outbreak of war in 1939 saw the takeover of large houses for storage, offices, reception centres and auxiliary hospitals and the commandeering of some for the billeting of troops. Evacuees were brought from danger zones as Dunham and Bowdon were considered to be safe areas, although most of them returned to their homes within a short time. Conscription took men, and later women, into the forces, farms were strictly controlled by the War Agricultural Committee and land improvements were put in hand. Farm workers were exempt from military service as farming was a reserved occupation and the Women's Land Army provided additional support.

Civil defence had already been competently organized in all aspects. It dealt with the air raids which took place on Altrincham in the winter of 1940-1941, the virtual destruction of the hamlet of Little Bollington and the razing of the entrance lodges to Dunham Massey Hall. Following the threat of invasion, Home Guard units were formed. Men were trained, outside working hours, in matters of defence in order to assist the armed forces had the need occurred. Some local Nazi sympathisers were arrested and suspected spies were interrogated. The upper park to Dunham Massey Hall was commandeered and converted into a military camp, which was used by American troops when their country entered the war. It was later used as a prisoner-of-war camp for the internment of Italian soldiers, followed by German and Austrian troops. The Italians were released to work on farms, after their country joined the Allies as co-belligerents, and they became very popular with local residents who found them very friendly and efficient workers.

Early in the war, Colonel Buckmaster, while reorganizing the Intelligence Services of the country, commandeered Dunham House as a training centre for Allied agents operating in occupied territory. These included Odette Churchill and Violette Szabo, both of whom received the George Cross for bravery.

Post-war mandatory local government master plans restricted development by landowners who were obliged to adhere to strict regulations. As an area of scenic and scientific interest, the Bollin Valley was scheduled as Green Belt. Most of the Stamford Estate was reserved for agriculture and

A guest at a Hall garden party celebrating the return of the Stamford family to Dunham Massey in 1906.

much of the remaining land, mainly owned by the Church Commissioners, became Grey Belt and reserved for release for residential development as the need arose. Shortage of building materials initially limited housebuilding, and strict licensing controls were introduced limiting cost and size. Design was greatly influenced by contemporary work in Sweden and the innovative effects of the Festival of Britain. The village of Bowdon was scheduled as a Conservation Area of Historical and Architectural interest.

New prosperity was brought to North Cheshire by the establishment of the United Kingdom Atomic Energy Authority and nuclear research centres at Risley Moss; the building of Warrington New Town; the development of the University of Manchester Institute of Science and Technology as a world centre; and the introduction of industries such as electronics. Aided by the building of the motorway system and Manchester International Airport, this attracted technocrats from every part of the world.

With the return of prosperity and increased affluence, some of the Victorian mansions were replaced by luxurious but more manageable dwellings with heated swimming pools, saunas and state-of-the-art equipment. Other mansions were converted into flats and retain their Victorian character. House prices rose, matching those in London for equivalent property, and social life flourished again as it had in the Victorian era.

The 10th Earl of Stamford, who never married, was disillusioned with post-war Britain and gradually became reclusive, living alone at the Hall with his mother. He was attended by non-resident staff and rarely left the confines of his estate. When he died in 1976, he bequeathed the Hall, its contents and the whole estate with endowment to the National Trust, who very carefully and conscientiously restored the Hall, the gardens and the deer park. Each year 120,000 visitors are attracted to the Hall and gardens and 500,000 visit the park. These and other efforts by the National Trust have made Dunham Massey a great award-winning showplace and a main centre for cultural activities and relaxation for a vast region, thus fulfilling the dreams of the former owners.

A group of women from Bowdon Vale assembled near the River Bollin.

The Countess of Stamford laying the foundation stone for the new school at Bowdon Vale.

The bowling green, Axe and Cleaver, Dunham Town. The clock face is thought to have come from the old infirmary at Piccadilly, Manchester.

This was a 1906 Belsize car belonging to the Okell family.

Left: Overley, Langham Road, the Okell residence. *Right:* Samuel Okell's observatory. Many Bowdon residents bought cars and built observatories at the end of the nineteenth century.

The Gaddum family car outside The Priory. The car, number M 2420, is an Austin Landaulette registered in 1909.

A chauffeur with a 40hp Daimler of 1905 in Bowdon.

Cheshire Yeomanry on the Devisdale in 1914.

Left: The Revd Hewlett-Johnson, vicar of St Margaret's and later the 'Red Dean' of Canterbury, provided spiritual help to German prisoners of war. *Right:* A 1917 insurance policy providing cover for air raid damage in Bowdon.

Local volunteers, *c.* 1916.

British Legion on Remembrance Day in Bowdon Vale, *c.* 1920.

The Bowdon Assembly Rooms were designed by the architect Frank Dunkerley, *c.* 1903.

Athelney, South Downs Road. A very fine example of a 'Dream House' from the Arts and Crafts movement.

Mr Betts, a one-armed RAC patrol man, on point duty in Chester Road.

A local motorcycle club at the Swan Hotel, Bucklow Hill. The motor car, registration number N 394, is a Di Dion of 1904.

Arthur and Katherine Hill (née Syers) leave the bride's family home, Rose Hill Cottage, East Downs Road, for their honeymoon after their wedding at Bowdon Church on 20 August 1914. The motor car, registration number M 6154, is possibly a Standard and is being driven by one of the bride's brothers, Alec, who is reputed to have accompanied the couple on their honeymoon. After the First World War Arthur Hill became a solicitor with a practice in Altrincham called Hill & Co. and in 1929 he became Mayor of Altrincham.

The wedding party at Rose Hill Cottage. Left to right: Miss A. Syers, Mr A. Syers, Mr F. Hill, Miss L. Syers.

The front elevation of Windy Ridge.

Windy Ridge, rear elevation. Built in the Arts and Crafts style to the design of F.H. Brazier, it became the vicarage after the Second World War. The house was built by Mr and Mrs Pearce.

John Leeming lands his plane on Chester Road to refuel near the Swan Hotel, Bucklow Hill, *c.* 1920. He was a founder member of the Lancashire Aero Club and flew the club's first aircraft on its debut flight from Alexandra Park, Manchester, in 1922. He lived in Bowdon and wrote several books including novels and some on gardening.

T.A. Coward, an eminent Bowdon field naturalist, in 1927.

A private residence in Bow Green Road designed in Lutyen's Kentish style with details copied from Great Dixter, *c.* 1929.

Local authority housing in Bowdon Vale, *c.* 1925. These are local houses designed by F.H. Brazier for both private and public sectors.

Altrincham High School for Girls, Bowdon, c. 1910.

In the centre is Miss Mary Howes-Smith, the headmistress, with staff and pupils, c. 1931. Other staff in the picture include: Miss Parker, Miss Mowson, Miss Hogg (First Assistant), Miss Coleman, Miss Hookins.

Altrincham High School for Boys, *c.* 1912.

In the centre is Mr Laver the headmaster with staff and pupils, *c.* 1930. The staff are: Mr Hale, Mr Hill, Mr Chorley, Mr Hamblin (First Assistant), Mr Mason, Mr Gough, Mr Gow, Mr Galloway.

Ronald Gow directing *The Glittering Sword*, a film made by the boys at the Altrincham County High School in 1928.

RONALD GOW — DRAMATIST
LIVED HERE 1898—1910
PUPIL & MASTER AT
ALTRINCHAM COUNTY HIGH FOR BOYS.
1937, MARRIED ACTRESS
DAME WENDY HILLER

SPONSORED BY BARCLAYS BANK PLC

One of the plaques that commemorate the life and work of Ronald Gow, the dramatist and educational film pioneer, who was a first year intake pupil and later a master at the Altrincham County High School.

Madge Atkinson (1885-1970) was the founder of the Natural Branch of the Imperial Society of Teachers of Dancing. In the 1920s she lived at Enville House, Bowdon. Brought up in Manchester in the atmosphere of the theatre (her father John Atkinson was a well-known Shakespearean actor), she was influenced by the work of Isadora Duncan. She began to develop her own method of training natural movement. In 1918 she opened her School of Natural Movement in Deansgate, Manchester, which had a curriculum offering training in all forms of dance. Among her many activities she was ballet mistress at Miss Horniman's Gaiety Theatre and arranged ballets for the Grand Opera Festivals held in the Manchester Opera House. She was honoured with a professorship at the Royal Manchester School of Music where she taught movement, mime and gesture to the student singers. In 1936, with partner Anita Heyworth, she moved her school to London. Evacuated to Devon during the war, she continued to teach at Dartford College, Kent, and later helped to form the London College of Dance and Drama. In recognition of her work she was awarded an Honorary Fellowship of the Imperial Society.

Boy Scouts, Dunham Massey Park, c. 1930.

Lord Baden-Powell being directed for a scout propaganda film that was produced by the Altrincham County High School for Boys in 1928.

The local scout clubhouse, 1932.

Scoutmasters Mr Vincent Brook, Mr H. Killick, Mr Hamblin and Mr R. Gow.

Hale Station in the 1900s. The locomotive is a Great Central Railway Sacré 0-6-0 of class '18', on a Northwich bound goods train. W.H. Smith's bookstall is on the left. The station was opened by the Cheshire Midland Railway on 12 May 1862 under the name of Bowdon Peel Causeway. Several name changes took place during the following forty years: Peel Causeway (Bowdon), Peel Causeway and Peel Causeway for Hale. It was enlarged in the 1880s and the name changed again to Hale in 1902, when the growing township needed better identification. It was restored after being made a Grade 2 listed building in 1984.

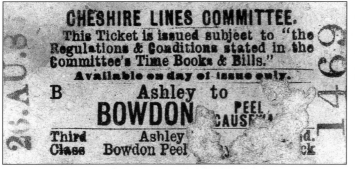

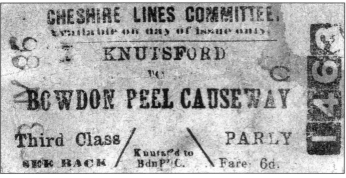

Tickets dated 1886 were found in the station during alterations in the 1970s. The 'parly' ticket (bottom left) was a result of Gladstone's Railway Act of 1884. This ruled that all railways sanctioned after that date must operate one train daily over each route. These trains would convey third-class passengers in enclosed carriages with roofs and windows, though some companies attempted to avoid providing the latter. Seating cost 1d per mile. Trains were to call at all stations and had a scheduled average speed of 12mph. Fares collected on these trains qualified for a remission of government duty.

Bowdon Bowling Club. Adolph Brodsky, who became a member in 1906, is seated second from right.

Gathering at the Altrincham County High School for Girls, *c.* 1930.

Bomb damage to lodge gates near Newbridge Hollow, Dunham Massey Park, 1940.

Destruction of Little Bollington village by enemy action, December 1940.

Dunham House, situated opposite the prisoner-of-war camp, Charcoal Road.

Colonel Maurice Buckmaster (left) set up a Special Operations Executive training centre for secret agents in Dunham House. These included Violette Szabo GC (right) and Odette Churchill GC.

British agents from Dunham House assist saboteurs in France, *c.* 1943.

Field Marshal Montgomery with the headmaster, Mr Hamblin, when he visited the County High School for Boys, *c.* 1944. The school was later renamed Altrincham Grammar School.

The Earl and dowager the Countess of Stamford entertained Emperor Haile Selassie during his exile in Britain. His arrival at the Hall was the last time the Newbridge Hollow drive was officially used.

Below left: A ration book. *Below right:* An advertisement for air raid wardens' entertainment.

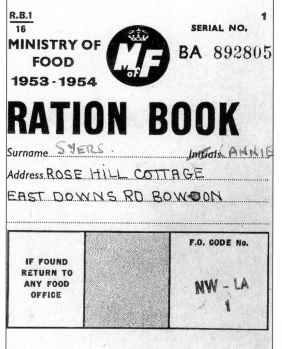

AIR-RAID WARDENS
OF
BOWDON WEST WARD

ENTERTAIN

Major FRANK HOWARD,

HEAD WARDEN, 1938-1945.

⎯ ・・ ・・ ⎯

ANGEL HOTEL,   Thursday,
KNUTSFORD.   31st. May, 1945.

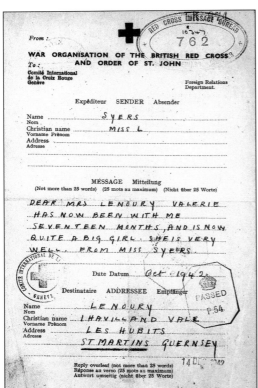

This is a Red Cross message dated October 1942. It was sent by Miss Lucy Syers of Rose Hill Cottage to Mrs Le Noury, the mother of Valerie, a Guernsey refugee that the Syers family were looking after. Today, Valerie Petit (née Le Noury) has happy memories of her time in Bowdon. She was eight years old on arrival and recalls the deer in Dunham Park; creeping from her bedroom to listen to 'beautiful classical music' played by a German maid called Ellie Fuch; Brendan, the hostel on The Firs; and the air raid shelter near the Assembly Rooms. Valerie went to Bowdon Church School. Les Vauxbelets College, a boys' school also from Guernsey, moved to Hale and then, in 1941, onto Oakleigh, Dunham Road, where it became the forerunner of St Ambrose College. One of the boys, Eric Clark, stayed on after the war and organized a successful reunion at the Bowdon Hotel in 1985. On Valerie's return home at the age of thirteen she became a hairdresser and married. She has two daughters, a son and five grandchildren.

Mrs Le Noury's reply, dated June 1943, which was on the reverse of the letter opposite.

Bowdon

URBAN DISTRICT OFFICIAL GUIDE

The

Assembly Rooms

THE FIRS — BOWDON

for a truly memorable function

and the

Richmond Suite

which is so ideal for the smaller party

Both are sumptuously appointed with excellent cuisine

The ideal venue for

BANQUETS · WEDDINGS · PARTIES · BUSINESS
CONFERENCES and all manner of Functions

Details from
The Manager, The Firs, Bowdon
Telephone 061-928 4049

Above left: This coat of arms comes from a local guide on Bowdon. *Above right:* The Assembly Rooms, The Firs, Bowdon. *Below:* An advertisement for Bowdon and Hale hand laundry. The proprietress was Mrs Richards.

BOWDON & HALE

HAND LAUNDRY

THE RED HOUSE, BOWDON.

A High-class
Modern
Laundry
dealing with
best Family
washings
only.

❀

Open-air
Drying a
special
feature
of the estab-
lishment.

The Cinema House in Willowtree Road, Altrincham, decorated for the Coronation of 1937. The poster advertises *Where There's a Will* with Will Hay, a popular comedian at the time. The cinema, which opened in 1923 and closed in 1978, now has flats standing on the site. Although situated in Altrincham, it adjoined the borders of Hale and Bowdon and later became known as Hale Cinema. It became a popular venue for patrons from the three districts and beyond and had the advantage of customers being able to book seats by telephone. Between the World Wars the café within the cinema became a meeting place for young people.

Professor Lord Bowden (no connection with Bowdon other than that of a resident), the former Minister of Technology and Principal of the University of Manchester Institute of Technology, in his garden in Stanhope Road, Bowdon. He was a leading technocrat who assisted in establishing the North-West as a world centre of technology.

Post-war housing in Bowdon.

A post-war bungalow in Bowdon. The design of houses in post-war Bowdon was influenced by Scandinavian architecture and the Festival of Britain in 1951. It was simple, elegant and well proportioned.

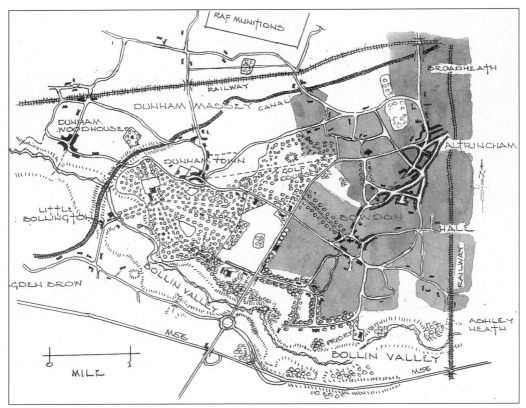

A sketch map of Bowdon and district at the end of the twentieth century.

The Altrincham Court Leet holds its Trinity Assize at Dunham Massey Hall in June 1998. Bryan Massey is the Steward to the Barony and John Tolley the Provost of Altrincham.

Earlscliffe, Devisdale Road. This was a new property built within a designated conservation area and designed to conform with existing development.

Bow Lane, Bowdon. Riding is a popular pursuit in Bowdon which has considerable facilities for equestrian activities.

The Gaddum family taking a stroll along Priory Road. Local authority houses were built on the west side of the road around 1925 (see p. 109). The Gaddums, who moved from Hale to Bowdon Priory, were local benefactors, and popular and influential residents. Mr H.T. Gaddum was unanimously elected chairman of the Bowdon Urban District Council on Monday 31 December 1894, following the dissolution of the local board on Friday 28 December that year. H.W. Evason was appointed Clerk of the Council and James Parnall as the Surveyor and Inspector of Public Nuisances. The following residents were elected as councillors on 15 December: John Alderley, John Ferguson, David Senior, Edward John Sidebottom, Samuel Wilkey Gillett, James Hall, Arthur Adlington Howorth, John Arthur Warburton, Fredrick George Whittall, Robert Wright Trenbath. Arthur Howorth held a ministerial post in Lloyd George's wartime Government for which he was awarded a baronetcy. His son, later Sir Geoffrey, was married to Dorothy Gaddum at Bowdon Parish Church by the Bishop of Chester in 1926.